BOOK ANALYSIS

By Benjamin Taylor

Pnin

by Vladimir Nabokov

VLADIMIR NABOKOV

RUSSIAN-AMERICAN NOVELIST

- **Born in St. Petersburg in 1899.**
- **Died in Montreux in 1977.**
- **Notable works:**
  - *Lolita* (1955), novel
  - *Pale Fire* (1962), novel
  - *Ada or Ardor: A Family Chronicle* (1969), novel

Born into an aristocratic Russian family in the late 19th century, Vladimir Nabokov would go on to become one of the foremost novelists of the 20th century. His family were forced to flee Russia after the 1917 October Revolution and he lived in Paris and Berlin as an exile, before moving to America in reaction to the looming danger of German occupation of France in the Second World War (1939-45) during the early 1940s. Nabokov was a renowned linguist, able to speak Russian, English and French fluently. He began writing in Russian, but it was not until he took up English – with novels such as the revered but controversial *Lolita* – that he began to achieve commercial and critical success. Nabokov is generally associated with innovative experiments with structure and plot, as well as with linguistic prowess, his prose boasting an elaborate use of metaphors, puns and stylish lyricism. Nabokov is the author of dozens of novels, short stories, poems and plays and was, in his time, also well regarded as an entomologist, becoming an expert in the study of butterflies.

PNIN

COLLEGIATE LIFE

- **Genre:** novel
- **Reference edition:** Nabokov, V. (2016) *Pnin*. London: Penguin Classics.
- **1st edition:** 1957
- **Themes:** literature, Russia, outsiderdom, memory, belonging, America, the past

Pnin was published in 1957, written in the wake of the success of Nabokov's most famous work, *Lolita*. It tells the story of a college professor and Russian émigré, Timofey Pnin, and his life teaching at Waindell College in the USA, drawing from Nabokov's own experiences as both a former Russian national and an American college professor at Cornell University and Wellesley College. It is Nabokov's 13th novel and was originally published in English, achieving widespread critical success and helping to transform Nabokov into one of the most admired novelists working in America at the time. Due to the highly personal nature of the novel, many of the characters and places dotted around the fictional Waindell College are said to be based on real life, with the character of Pnin, for example, rumoured to be inspired by Marc Szeftel, a colleague of Nabokov's and fellow Russian émigré. Despite being dwarfed by the mainstream success of *Lolita,* which is widely considered one of the greatest novels of the last century, *Pnin* is well-regarded by critics and considered one of Nabokov's most important works.

SUMMARY

THE WRONG TRAIN

We are introduced to Professor Timofey Pnin sitting in a carriage on the wrong train, *not* on his way to give a Friday evening lecture at the Cremona Women's Club, which is over 200km west of his own university, Waindell, at which he teaches Russian language and literature. He realises his mistake when he converses with the conductor and leaves the train at the next stop.

The next stop is a town called Whitchurch, and at the station Pnin finds that there is a four o' clock bus departing in a matter of minutes. He leaves his bag at the station with one of the employees and goes to a café, only to return to find a different employee who cannot authorise the return of his bag. In blind haste, Pnin rushes to catch the bus, deciding to leave his possessions behind in order to make his appointment on time. A few minutes later, however, he realises that he has left his lecture – which he prefers to read straight from the paper – in his bag and must get off the bus to retrieve it. He sits and despairs on a bench and imagines that he is having a heart attack. His mind casts back to when he was sick as a child in St. Petersburg.

Despite everything that has happened, Pnin manages to get a lift in a truck and arrives on time to the event and imagines that he sees several individuals from his past alive in the hall watching him at the dinner.

A RETURNING FACE

Mr and Mrs Clements receive a call from Professor Pnin, who is interested in taking up their spare room. He soon arrives to inspect the place and takes the room, moving his possessions in with the help of one of his car-owning students. Things go well in his new residence, Pnin finding fuel for his love of gadgets with the endlessly turning washing machine and developing a burgeoning friendship with the Clements. He gets his teeth removed and replaced with dentures and enjoys their superior effectiveness. One day, he is startled to receive a letter informing him that his former wife, Dr Liza Wind, is to visit him at the house.

Liza met Pnin in Paris in the 20s, where they married, though it is revealed that she left him for Dr Victor Wind, a fellow psychologist, whom she married and bore a son in America. Pnin is nervous and excited on learning the news of her coming in a clear sign of his residual infatuation with her. When she arrives at the house, however, Pnin is dismayed at her cruel and indifferent attitude towards him and finds that the reason she has come is to ask him to provide pocket money for her son, Victor, who is to attend an expensive private school. Victor is a unique child of 14, who has exasperated his two parents by what seems like an imperviousness to psychoanalysis and a keen aptitude for art. Pnin soon starts a correspondence with the boy who comes to visit the old professor during his holidays.

THE SUMMER

We next join Pnin several months later on his way to a friend's country house for the summer. The house, which belongs to Alexandr Petrovich Kukolnikov (known as 'Al Cook'), is filled with fellow Russian émigrés, including Pnin's great friend from the University of Prague, Chateau.

Pnin spends his time playing chess, talking with his friends and dominating games of croquet. However, one of the women he meets reminds him of his childhood sweetheart, Mira, whom he lost contact with and who was killed in a concentration camp during the Second World War.

PNIN'S DOWNFALL

Back in Waindell, the Fall term is starting and Pnin has found a perfectly suitable house in which he continues to do his research. Little does he know that Professor Hagen, who heads his department, has been offered a job at another college and is troubled by what will happen to Pnin, who is unpopular in the modern languages department and unwanted by many of his colleagues. Meanwhile, the oblivious Pnin decides to throw a housewarming party, and invites several of his college associates, including Hagen and the Clements. Towards the end of the party, Pnin expresses his delight at his new house and breaks the news that he plans to purchase it, predicting that he will soon get tenure. Professor Hagen reveals to him, however, that he is effectively fired, with the one unnamed professor who would take Pnin and his Russian classes turning out to be someone whom Pnin refuses to work with.

The final chapter of the book details the narrator's own relationship to Pnin, his memories of meeting him at several stages in his childhood in Russia and adult life in Paris and New York, and the revelation that he is the new professor tasked with taking the reins of the Russian division of the modern language department. Each time the narrator met with Pnin, the old professor would vehemently deny having really known him, and the narrator is hurt when he receives a letter from Pnin telling him that he does not wish to work under him, and that he has rejected the teaching profession altogether. When the narrator arrives in Waindell, he rings up Pnin, who puts on a fake voice and claims to be long gone. The novel ends with the narrator witnessing Pnin driving his car, which is packed with all of his possessions, speedily into the distance.

CHARACTERS

PROFESSOR TIMOFEY PNIN

Professor Pnin, known casually as Pnin throughout, is the eponymous protagonist of the novel, and teaches Russian language and literature at Waindell College in the USA. A Russian émigré who fled from "Leninized Russia" (p. 1) in the 1920s, Pnin is a strange and oft-ridiculed figure, separated from his peers by his bizarre eccentricities and the ongoing nature of his American naturalisation. He is described from the outset as "Ideally bald, sun-tanned, and clean shaven, he began rather impressively with that great brown dome of his, tortoise-shell glasses (masking an infantile absence of eyebrows), apish upper lip, thick neck, and strong-man torso in a tightish tweed coat, but ended, somewhat disappointingly , in a pair of spindly legs" (*ibid.*), a man who, "despite his many shortcomings, had about him a disarming, old-fashioned charm" (p. 4). Pnin is defined by his physical awkwardness and an almost fanatical knowledge and academic passion for Russian literature and culture. He does, however, come alive in certain environments, when playing croquet for example: "the man was transfigured. From his habitual, slow, ponderous, rather rigid self-, he changed into a terrifically mobile, scampering, mute, sly-visaged hunchback" (p. 113).

Due to his lack of friends, estrangement from his ex-wife Liza, with whom he is clearly still infatuated, and tragic and sometimes haunting past, Pnin is generally depicted as an isolated figure. This is accentuated by his status as an émigré, struggling at times in engagement with his new home: "America, my new country, wonderful America which sometimes surprises me but always provokes respect" (p. 89). As such, Pnin strikes a nomadic figure in the novel, often having to move to and from temporary accommodation in a situation that symbolises the precariousness of life as a foreign national. This is indeed plain to see at the end of the novel, when, having finally found a suitable house, Pnin finds out that he has been fired and is forced to move away.

LIZA WIND

The former wife of Pnin (and as such formerly Liza Pnin), Liza Wind appears intermittently in Pnin's life and memories. She met and married him in Paris in the 1920s while studying for a psychology degree, before leaving him for another psychologist called Dr Eric Wind, with whom she had a child, Victor. Liza appears without warning in Pnin's life in the novel, coming to visit him at Waindell and asking him to fund Victor's expenses while he attends boarding school. It is also revealed during this visit that her marriage with Eric is breaking up, and a clear transferral of paternal responsibilities over Victor seems to pass to Pnin, who begins a correspondence with the boy, inviting him to stay with him at Waindell.

Liza is, outside of her fleeting visit, largely defined by Pnin's attitude towards her. He is clearly still infatuated with her, and as such there is a distinct contrast between the Liza of his memories and the real Liza. For example, she is described as having "hardly a flaw to her full-blown, animated, elemental, not particularly well-groomed beauty" (p. 34) and is associated with a sugar-coated almond: "remained in his mind, forever mingled with the memory of her taut skin, her complexion, her flawless teeth" (p. 37). However, once she comes to visit and insults his accommodation and job before coercing him into funding her son's amusement, a wholly different picture of her emerges: "her cruelty, with her vulgarity, with her blinding blue eyes, with her miserable poetry, with her fat feet, with her impure, dry, sordid, infantile soul" (p. 47).

VICTOR WIND

Victor is the son of Eric and Liza Wind, a teenage boy of extreme artistic ability of whom the narrator claims "I do not think he loved anybody" (p. 73). He strikes an isolated figure in the novel, without particular attachment to either parent, and as such seems to bond instinctively with Pnin when he goes to visit the old professor during half term at his boarding school. He is reportedly highly intelligent and is apparently unfazed by unfamiliar situations. The narrator claims that he has "a casual ease of demeanour, an expression of amiable aloofness about his plain but clean-cut features, and a complete lack of clumsiness or constraint which, far from precluding modest and reserve, lent a sunny something to his shyness and a detached blandness to his quiet ways" (p. 73). Victor is defined in the novel by the semi-contradiction between his artistic talent and an extreme lack of unconventionality. Indeed, his psychologist parents are displeased by his eschewing of psycho-analytical stereotypes: "to the Winds, Victor was a problem child insofar as he refused to be one. From the Winds' point of view, every male child had an ardent desire to castrate his father and a nostalgic urge to re-enter his mother's body. But Victor did not reveal any behaviour disorder, did not pick his nose, did not suck his thumb, was not even a nail-biter" (p. 76). In this sense Victor is abnormal, simply by the perfection of his normality.

THE NARRATOR

The narrator of *Pnin* emerges as a character more and more as the plot develops, to the point that the final chapter contains a detailed account of the various times he has met Pnin during his lifetime – firstly in Russia as children, but also in

Paris and New York. Pnin has a strange aversion to the narrator, however, refusing to work with him in the department of modern languages, and notably denying the truth of his stories of their partially shared childhoods. As such, we come to question the reliability of the narrator's account of the life and times of Timofey Pnin, as well as the nature of their relationship, with the narrator's own association with Pnin appearing to change throughout: "Was his seizure a heart attack? I doubt it. For the nonce I am his physician, and let me repeat, I doubt it" (p. 13). The reality of the story of *Pnin* becomes increasingly unclear and it comes to seem more like the omniscient narrator's construction, something which Pnin himself seems to react to by refusing to work with him when he is hired by Waindell College and evading him at the end of the novel.

ANALYSIS

MEMORY

One of the major themes in *Pnin* is that of memory, and the effect that the resonance of the past has on the novel's protagonist as he goes through his life. It is clear that Pnin has had a difficult past defined by his escape from the Bolshevik Russia of the early 20th century, his failed marriage to Liza and the death of friends and his childhood sweetheart Mira. Throughout the novel, he comes across what seem like accidental memory associations, where certain situations remind him of his past, and we experience an actualisation of his memory, where the present and the past seem to merge in Pnin's head. One instance of this occurs when he goes to give a guest lecture at the Cremona Women's Club: "in the middle of the front row of the seats he saw one of his Baltic aunts, wearing the pearls and the lace and the blonde wig she had worn at all the performances given by the great ham actor Khodotov... Murdered, forgotten, unrevenged, incorrupt, immortal, many old friends were scattered throughout the dim hall" (p. 19).

He has a similar experience in the college library when "for no special reason the reader suddenly saw, with passionate and ridiculous lucidity his parents... sitting in two armchairs, facing each other in a small, cheerfully lighted drawing room on Galernaya Street, St Petersburg, forty years ago" (p. 63). In the creation of this surreal space where memory and reality merge, Nabokov is attempting to represent the internal experience of memory, where remembered encounters with the past are given equal footing with the experiences of real life. The consistent, involuntary recollections to which Pnin is subject throughout the novel furthermore make him out to be a man haunted by sections of his past, with talk of Mira in particular affecting him negatively as a result of her tragic death at the hands of the Nazis: "In order to exist rationally, Pnin had taught himself, during the last ten years, never to remember Mira Belochkin" (p. 117).

LANGUAGE

Vladimir Nabokov is often associated with an innovative and playful treatment of language. He was notably trilingual, and as such often plays with and makes fun of the intricate differences and similarities between various Western languages. His use of language in *Pnin* also comes from the perspective of a foreign national with a developing grasp on the colloquial use of English in America, a perspective with which he is able to explore the literalness of translation and the pitfalls of pronunciation. The approach to language in the novel is therefore often didactic as Pnin muddles his way through situations with a perfectly valid but not fully naturalised English, phonetically describing certain names, for example: "the once famous revolutionary Umov (rhymes with 'zoom off')" (p. 14). Indeed, a sort of hybrid language which combines English and Russian pronunciations emerges in the novel, known throughout as 'Pnin English' – itself a pun on 'pidgin English'; a simplified form of linguistic communication. For example, the narrator claims of him that "if his Russian was music, his English was murder. He had enormous difficulty ('dzeefeecooltsee' in Pninian English) with depalletization, never managing to remove the extra Russian moisture from *t*'s and *d*'s" (p. 54). He even manages to identify Pnin by his voice, for "not even his best imitator could rhyme so emphatically 'at' with the German '*hat*', 'home' with the French *'homme'*, and 'gone' with the head of 'Goneril'" (p. 167). Pnin's English is a contorted amalgamation of European languages that is, despite its apparent erroneousness, vibrant and eclectic, as can be seen in the descriptions of his New York home "between Tsentral Park and Reeverside" (p. 51).

We can also find humour in Nabokov's approach to colloquialisms, with Pnin's literal translations dotted throughout the text, the narrator saying, for example: "the cat, as Pnin would say, cannot be hid in a bag" (p. 33). Nabokov's use of language is diverse and rich in its precise and often improvised vocabulary and syntax. Language furthermore plays a huge symbolic role in *Pnin*, as something which is universal and yet also exclusionary – the source of social cohesion and of misinterpretation which dominates the life of a man living in a foreign country.

OUTSIDERDOM AND FOREIGNNESS

Throughout the novel, things never seem to quite go right for Pnin. He gets on the wrong trains, misses buses, is kicked out of accommodation and perpetually left to wait by friends and relatives. He is dogged by an outsider status, symbolic of his peculiarity and identity as both a foreign national and a political exile, with the themes of outsiderdom that run through *Pnin* representing the isolated and often misunderstood life of its protagonist. Indeed, misinterpreted and falsified likenesses of Pnin are common throughout the novel. He is cruelly and excessively mimicked by a friend of the narrator in the final chapter in a bid to make fun of him, and indeed reportedly misrepresented by the narrator himself – who is angrily remonstrated with by Pnin, who accuses him of telling lies about their childhood in Russia. This cements Pnin's role as an outsider in the way that it shows how he is made into a caricature due to his inability to fully integrate on a cultural level. His identity is instead distorted and defined by others.

A recurring issue *Pnin* is Pnin's role as an exile, with Nabokov likely drawing from his own experiences, having fled from his native Russia as a child with his mother and father following the 1917 October Revolution. Pnin arrives in America from Paris in order to make a new start but is seemingly forever haunted by his past and unable to settle anywhere for very long. We can see this in the way that memory strikes him, almost like an attack in the novel, with faces from his past hounding him as he attempts to navigate collegiate life. It is as though, despite his physical extraction from the scenes of his youth, he is unable to escape from them. At one point he even suffers a nightmare concerning the pressures of Bolshevik Russian life: "one of those dreams that still haunt Russian fugitives, even when a third of a century has elapsed since their escape from the Bolsheviks, Pnin saw himself fantastically cloaked, fleeing through great pools of ink under a cloud-barred moon from a chimera palace, and then pacing a desolate strand with his dead friend Ilya Isidorovich Polyanski" (p. 94). Pnin's perennial outsiderdom is further represented in his lack of a home in the novel, as he moves from temporary accommodation to temporary accommodation, forever having to move on for some unfortunate reason. Pnin therefore remains, despite his attempts to settle at Waindell, nomadic and exiled to the end, unable to wholly adjust to his new environment as a result of the chains that connect him to his old one.

FURTHER REFLECTION

SOME QUESTIONS TO THINK ABOUT...

- Nabokov is well-known for his playful linguistic style. How do you think the way Nabokov writes differs from other writers?
- What can we tell about Nabokov's attitude to his native Russia from *Pnin*?
- Think of some of the recurring symbols in *Pnin* – such as that of the squirrel which confronts Pnin seemingly everywhere he goes. What do you think it means?
- Do you think that Nabokov accurately represents the experience of memory in the novel? Explain your answer.
- Do you think that Pnin is treated differently because of his foreignness? Explain your answer.
- How does Nabokov successfully depict the life of a foreign national living in America? Consider what it would be like to live in a foreign country.
- To what extent is language the greatest barrier for Pnin in the novel? What else do you think causes his isolation?

- Consider the plot of *Pnin*. Is it a conventional one? Is there an enfolding story or are the chapters disjointed and episodic? Why do you think Nabokov has done this?

We want to hear from you!
Leave a comment on your online library
and share your favourite books on social media!

FURTHER READING

REFERENCE EDITION

- Nabokov, V. (2016) *Pnin*. London: Penguin Classics.

MORE FROM BRIGHTSUMMARIES.COM

- Reading guide – *Lolita* by Vladimir Nabokov.
- Reading guide – *Pale Fire* by Vladimir Nabokov.

www.brightsummaries.com

Ebook EAN: 9782808019460

Paperback EAN: 9782808019477

Legal Deposit: D/2019/12603/140

Cover: © Primento

Digital conception by Primento, the digital partner of publishers.